craving
cookies

Chef
express

Published by:
TRIDENT REFERENCE PUBLISHING
801 12th Avenue South, Suite 400
Naples, Fl 34102 USA

Tel: + 1 (239) 649-7077
www.tridentreference.com
email: sales@tridentreference.com

craving
cookies

Craving Cookies
© TRIDENT REFERENCE PUBLISHING

Publisher
Simon St. John Bailey

Editor-in-chief
Susan Knightley

Prepress
Precision Prep & Press

Includes Index
ISBN 1582796793
UPC 6 15269 96793 5

Printed in The United States

introduction

In this book you will find such a wonderful array of cookies, that you will find easy to understand why this type of baked product is so popular: they are not only easy to make, but also come in a huge variety of flavors and textures, and they are just the right size for a snack.

craving cookies
introduction

Homemade biscuits and cookies have special appeal with their tempting aromas and flavors. Some of our sweet ones are splendidly rich; others are simpler but not less delicious. There's a savory section, as well, with unmissable tasty bites to enjoy.

- Smooth chocolate, chunky chocolate, lots and lots of chocolate, carob and coffee treats are all here for your pleasure, in sweet delights to serve after dinner or at any time.

- Crunchy morsels of flavor, nuts and seeds also contain good oils that make them high in nutritional value. If you prefer to use your own favorite nuts, substitute an equivalent amount for the quantity given in any of our recipes.

- The great thing about macaroons is that you get heaps for your money, and they will be perfect every time if you make sure the sugar is dissolved in the egg white before cooking. When cooked correctly, macaroons will keep in an airtight container for weeks, ready to

dress up when you want a specially glamorous treat. They're also great used as the base or topping for quick and easy desserts. So never throw away an egg white; whisk it to bliss!

- Multi-function coconut's greatest asset is that it goes so well with everything. It mixes easily with nuts, chocolate, spices, fruit (particularly lemon), whatever you like best. As well as flavor, it lends a tender moistness to biscuits and slices, which usually keep well as a result.

- There are many delicious things to chew on in crunchy biscuits and cookies enriched with the natural goodness of cereals. Some are smart and many will become nutritious stand-bys for packed lunches. A bonus with cereals is that they are a great source of dietary fiber.

- Tasty bites like the ones we present are terrific to have on hand to serve with drinks or for family eating. The savory tastes will be popular with kids and adults alike.

Difficulty scale

■☐☐ I Easy to do

■■☐ I Requires attention

■■■ I Requires experience

cinnamon crisps

■□□ | Cooking time: 10 minutes - Preparation time: 10 minutes

method

1. Place butter and ³/₄ cup/170 g/5¹/₂ oz sugar in a bowl and beat until light and fluffy. Add egg and beat well.

2. Sift together plain flour, self-raising flour and bicarbonate of soda and stir into butter mixture. Turn dough onto a floured surface and knead briefly. Wrap in plastic food wrap and refrigerate for 30 minutes or until firm.

3. Place cinnamon and remaining sugar in a small bowl and mix to combine. Roll dough into small balls, then roll balls in sugar mixture and place 5 cm/2 in apart on lightly greased baking trays. Bake at 180°C/350°F/Gas 4 for 8 minutes or until golden. Remove to wire racks to cool.

....
Makes 25

ingredients

> **125 g/4 oz butter**
> **1 cup/220 g/7 oz caster sugar**
> **1 egg**
> **1 cup/125 g/4 oz plain flour**
> **¹/₂ cup/60 g/2 oz self-raising flour**
> **¹/₂ teaspoon bicarbonate of soda**
> **2 teaspoons ground cinnamon**

tip from the chef

Fat or shortening in whatever form makes a baked product tender and helps to improve its keeping quality. In most baked goods, top quality margarine and butter are interchangeable.

basic biscuit recipe

■□□ | Cooking time: 15 minutes - Preparation time: 10 minutes

ingredients

> **125 g butter**
> **3/4 cup/185 g/6 oz caster sugar**
> **1 teaspoon vanilla essence**
> **1 egg**
> **1 cup/125 g/4 oz plain flour, sifted**
> **1 cup/125 g/4 oz self-raising flour, sifted**

method

1. Cream butter, sugar and vanilla until light and fluffy. Add egg and beat well.
   Fold in plain and self-raising flours, cover and refrigerate for 2 hours.
2. Roll heaped teaspoonfuls of mixture into balls. Place onto a greased oven tray, spacing well apart to allow for spreading. Flatten each biscuit slightly with a fork and bake at 180°C/350°F/Gas 4 for 12-15 minutes or until golden brown. Allow to cool on tray for a few minutes then transfer to a wire rack to finish cooling.

....
Makes 40

tip from the chef

Try these easy variations:

* *Spicy fruit cookies: Replace 4 tablespoons of the caster sugar with 4 tablespoons brown sugar. Sift 2 teaspoons cinnamon, 1 teaspoon mixed spice and 1 teaspoon ground ginger with the flour. Roll out mixture and cut 16 rounds. Place teaspoonfuls of fruit mince on half the rounds and cover with remaining rounds. Press edges lightly to seal and bake for 20-25 minutes.*

* *Three-chocolate cookies: Add 40 g/1 1/2 oz each finely chopped dark chocolate, milk chocolate and white chocolate to mixture after beating in the egg. Place spoonfuls of mixture on greased tray and bake as directed.*

* *Creamy jam drops: Roll mixture into balls and flatten slightly. Make indents in the center of each round, fill with a little cream cheese and top with a teaspoon jam. Bake as directed.*

coffee kisses

■■□ | Cooking time: 12 minutes - Preparation time: 10 minutes

ingredients
> 250 g/8 oz butter, softened
> 2/3 cup/100 g/3 1/2 oz icing sugar, sifted
> 2 teaspoons instant coffee powder dissolved in 1 tablespoon hot water, cooled
> 2 cups/250 g/8 oz flour, sifted
> 45 g/1 1/2 oz dark chocolate, melted
> extra icing sugar to dust

method
1. Place butter and icing sugar in a large mixing bowl and beat until light and fluffy. Stir in coffee mixture and flour.
2. Spoon mixture into a piping bag fitted with a medium star nozzle (a) and pipe 2 cm/3/4 in rounds of mixture 2 cm/3/4 in apart on greased baking trays (b). Bake at 180°C/350°F/Gas 4 for 10-12 minutes or until lightly browned. Stand on trays for 5 minutes before removing to wire racks to cool completely.
3. Join biscuits with a little melted chocolate (c), then dust with icing sugar.

....
Makes 25

tip from the chef
These charming cookies are ideal for serving with a nice tea in the afternoon, or a good coffee after dinner.

a

b

c

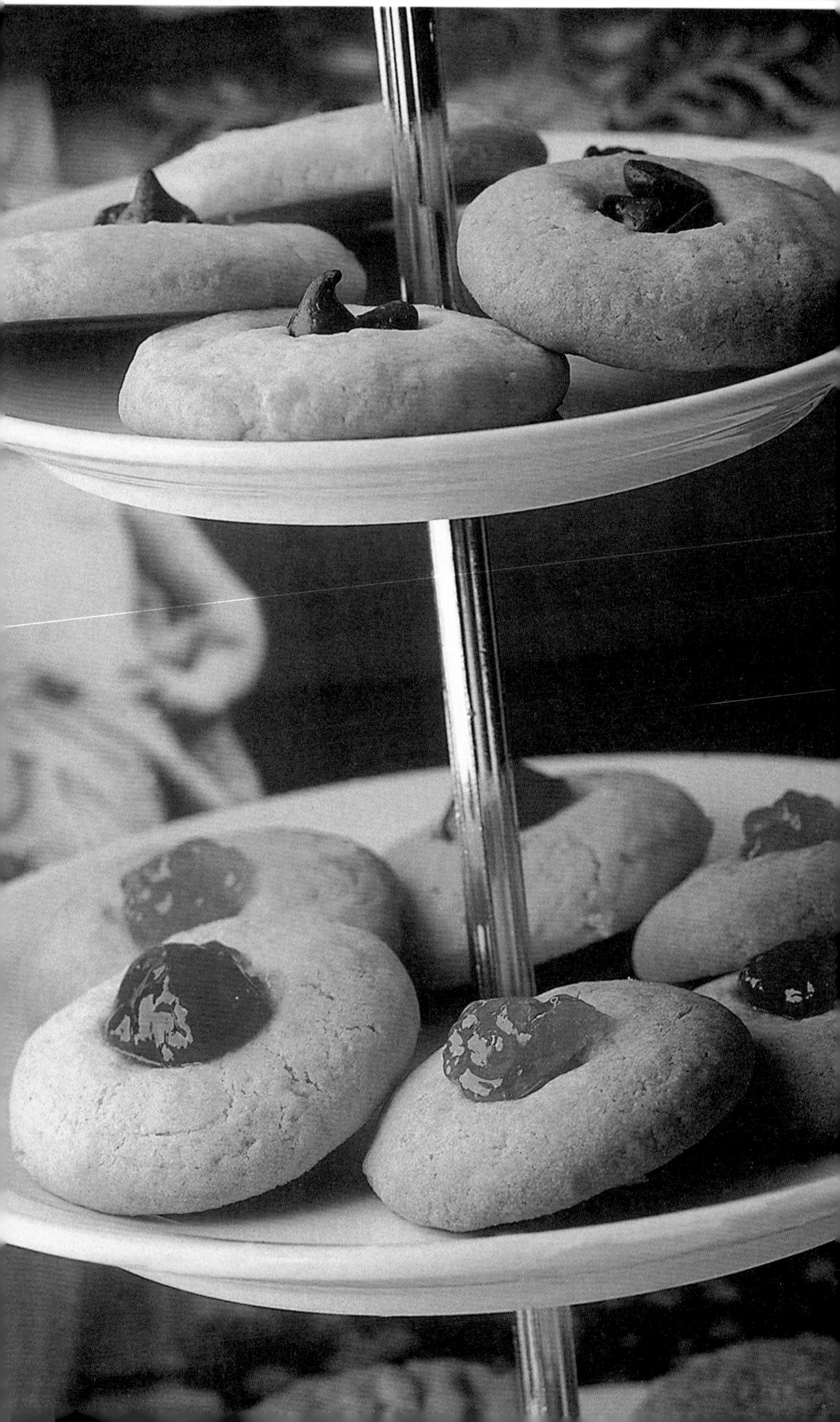

thumb
print cookies

■□□ I Cooking time: 15 minutes - Preparation time: 10 minutes

method

1. Place butter, icing sugar and vanilla essence in a bowl and beat until light and fluffy. Sift together plain flour, self-raising flour and custard powder. Fold flour mixture and milk, alternately, into butter mixture.
2. Roll tablespoons of mixture into balls and place on greased baking trays. Make a thumb print in the center of each cookie.
3. Fill thumb print hole with a teaspoon of jam, lemon curd or chocolate.
   Bake at 190°C/375°F/Gas 5 for 12 minutes or until cookies are golden. Transfer to wire racks to cool.

Makes 30

ingredients

> **185 g/6 oz butter, softened**
> **$1/3$ cup/45 g/$1^{1}/2$ oz icing sugar, sifted**
> **1 teaspoon vanilla essence**
> **$1/2$ cup/60 g/2 oz plain flour**
> **1 cup/125 g/4 oz self-raising flour**
> **$1/2$ cup/60 g/2 oz custard powder**
> **$1/4$ cup/60 ml/2 fl oz milk**
> **jam, lemon curd or chopped chocolate**

tip from the chef

Wrap the dough in plastic food wrap and chill at least 30 minutes to make it easier to shape into balls. For a subtle toasty nut flavor, roll the balls in sesame seeds before making the thumb print and filling.

night
sky cookies

■□□ | Cooking time: 10 minutes - Preparation time: 10 minutes

method

1. Place butter, sugar and almond essence in a bowl and beat until light and fluffy. Gradually beat in egg.
2. Sift together flour and baking powder (a). Fold flour mixture and milk, alternately, into butter mixture and mix to form a soft dough.
3. Roll out dough on a lightly floured surface to 5 mm/1/4 in thick. Using a star and a moon-shaped cookie cutter, cut out cookies (b). Place cookies on lightly greased baking trays and bake at 190°C/375°F/Gas 5 for 10 minutes or until cookies are golden and cooked. Transfer to wire racks to cool.
4. Dip tops of moon-shaped cookies in white chocolate and tips of star-shaped cookies in dark chocolate (c). Place on wire racks to set.

ingredients

> **125 g/4 oz butter, softened**
> **3/4 cup/170 g/51/2 oz caster sugar**
> **1/2 teaspoon almond essence**
> **1 egg, lightly beaten**
> **2 cups/250 g/8 oz flour**
> **1/2 teaspoon baking powder**
> **1/4 cup/60 ml/2 fl oz milk**
> **90 g/3 oz white chocolate, melted**
> **125 g/4 oz dark chocolate, melted**

Makes 24

tip from the chef

As an alternative, brush the cookies with beaten egg and sprinkle with sugar before baking.

a

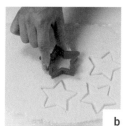
b

c

wholemeal
carob chip cookies

■□□ | Cooking time: 10 minutes - Preparation time: 10 minutes

ingredients
> **185 g/6 oz butter**
> **1¹/2 cup wholemeal
> self-raising flour**
> **¹/2 cup raw sugar**
> **90 g/3 oz carob, chopped**
> **1 egg, lightly beaten**

method
1. Rub butter into flour, using fingertips, until mixture resembles fine breadcrumbs. Stir in sugar and carob. Add egg, stir with a knife until just combined, knead lightly until smooth.
2. Roll out to 5 mm/¹/4 in thick on a lightly floured surface. Cut into circles using a 5 cm/2 in cutter. Place onto a lightly greased baking tray. Mark with prongs of a fork.
3. Bake in moderate oven 10 minutes or until golden brown, place on wire rack to cool. Store in airtight container.

Makes about 24

tip from the chef
It is important to use cold butter. For it to integrate quickly, dice it into small cubes.

golden
oat biscuits

■☐☐ | Cooking time: 15 minutes - Preparation time: 5 minutes

method

1. Place rolled oats, flour, coconut and sugar in a large bowl. Combine golden syrup, butter, water and bicarbonate of soda. Pour golden syrup mixture into dry ingredients and mix well to combine.

2. Drop teaspoons of mixture 3 cm/1¹/₄ in apart on greased baking trays and bake at 180°C/350°F/Gas 4 for 10-15 minutes or until biscuits are just firm. Stand on trays for 3 minutes before transferring to wire racks to cool.

....
Makes 30

ingredients

> **1 cup/90 g/3 oz rolled oats**
> **1 cup/125 g/4 oz flour, sifted**
> **90 g/3 oz desiccated coconut**
> **1 cup/250 g/8 oz sugar**
> **4 teaspoons golden syrup, warmed**
> **125 g/4 oz butter, melted**
> **2 tablespoons boiling water**
> **1 teaspoon bicarbonate of soda**

tip from the chef

Biscuits should always be stored in an airtight container. Allow the biscuits to cool completely on wire cooling racks before storing.

carob
hazelnut macaroons

■□□ I Cooking time: 15 minutes - Preparation time: 10 minutes

ingredients
> **2 eggs, separated**
> **185 g/6 oz caster sugar**
> **2 tablespoons carob powder, sifted**
> **250 g/8 oz desiccated coconut**
> **60 g/2 oz roasted hazelnuts, finely chopped**
> **100 g/3^1/$_2$ oz carob, melted**

method
1. Whisk egg whites until soft peaks form. Add sugar, a spoonful at a time, beating well after each addition, until mixture is of meringue consistency.
2. Beat egg yolks with carob powder and lightly fold through egg white mixture. Stir in coconut and hazelnuts.
3. Drop tablespoons of mixture onto greased oven trays and bake at 180°C/350°F/ Gas 4 for 15 minutes or until firm. Cool on trays. Drizzle with carob.

....
Makes 30

tip from the chef
Carob and hazelnuts combine to make a deliciously new version of an old favorite.

montecarlo
biscuits

■□□ | Cooking time: 15 minutes - Preparation time: 10 minutes

method

1. Place butter, brown sugar and vanilla essence in a bowl and beat until light and fluffy. Add egg, plain flour, self-raising flour, coconut and rolled oats (a) and mix well to combine.

2. Roll tablespoons of mixture into balls, place on greased baking trays and flatten slightly with a fork (b). Bake at 190°C/375°F/Gas 5 for 12 minutes or until biscuits are golden. Transfer to wire racks to cool.

3. To make butter cream, place butter, icing sugar and vanilla essence in a bowl and beat until light and fluffy. Spread half the biscuits with raspberry jam and top with butter cream (c). Top with remaining biscuits.

Makes 20

ingredients

> **125 g/4 oz butter, softened**
> **1 cup/170 g/5 1/2 oz brown sugar**
> **2 teaspoons vanilla essence**
> **1 egg, lightly beaten**
> **1 cup/125 g/4 oz plain flour, sifted**
> **1/2 cup/60 g/2 oz self-raising flour, sifted**
> **90 g/3 oz desiccated coconut**
> **3/4 cup/75 g/2 1/2 oz rolled oats**
> **1/2 cup/155 g/5 oz raspberry jam**

butter cream
> **60 g/2 oz butter, softened**
> **1/2 cup/75 g/2 1/2 oz icing sugar**
> **1 teaspoon vanilla essence**

tip from the chef

For the biscuits not to moisten, fill them at the last moment.

a

b

c

chocky road biscuits

■□□ | Cooking time: 10 minutes - Preparation time: 10 minutes

ingredients

> 250 g/8 oz butter, softened
> 1 cup/170 g/5 1/2 oz brown sugar
> 2 eggs, lightly beaten
> 3 cups/375 g/12 oz flour
> 1 cup/100 g/3 1/2 oz cocoa powder
> 1/4 cup/60 ml/2 fl oz buttermilk or milk
> 155 g/5 oz white chocolate, roughly chopped
> 90 g/3 oz peanuts, roasted
> 185 g/6 oz chocolate chips

method

1. Place butter and sugar in a bowl and beat until light and fluffy. Gradually beat in eggs.
2. Sift together flour and cocoa powder. Add flour mixture, milk, chocolate, peanuts and chocolate chips to egg mixture and mix well to combine.
3. Drop tablespoons of mixture onto lightly greased baking trays and bake at 180°C/350°F/Gas 4 for 10 minutes or until biscuits are cooked. Transfer to wire racks to cool.

....

Makes 36

tip from the chef

Peanuts and chocolate chips must be the two most favorite additions to any biscuit designed for kids.

giant
choc chip cookies

| Cooking time: 25 minutes - Preparation time: 10 minutes

method

1. Place butter, brown sugar, caster sugar and vanilla essence in a bowl and beat until light and fluffy. Gradually beat in eggs. Add flour, baking powder and chocolate chips and mix until just combined.
2. Place 3 tablespoons of mixture in piles well apart onto greased baking trays. Bake at 160°C/325°F/Gas 3 for 25 minutes or until golden, cool on wire racks.

....
Makes 24

ingredients

> **300 g/9^1/$_2$ oz butter, softened**
> **1^1/$_4$ cups/220 g/7 oz brown sugar**
> **^{2}/$_3$ cup/140 g/4^1/$_2$ oz caster sugar**
> **2 teaspoons vanilla essence**
> **2 eggs, lightly beaten**
> **3^1/$_4$ cups/410 g/13 oz flour, sifted**
> **1 teaspoon baking powder, sifted**
> **375 g/12 oz chocolate chips**

tip from the chef

Here's one for the school lunch box! For something different you might like to use white or milk chocolate chips or a mixture of dark, milk and white chocolate chips.

rich
choc chip cookies

■□□ | Cooking time: 15 minutes - Preparation time: 10 minutes

ingredients

> **125 g/4 oz butter**
> **1 cup/220 g/7 oz caster sugar**
> **1 egg, lightly beaten**
> **2 teaspoons vanilla essence**
> **1/4 cup/60 ml/2 fl oz milk**
> **1 1/4 cups/155 g/5 oz flour**
> **1/2 teaspoon bicarbonate of soda**
> **90 g/3 oz roasted hazelnuts, chopped**
> **125 g/4 oz chocolate chips**
> **90 g/3 oz shredded coconut**
> **90 g/3 oz sultanas**
> **90 g/3 oz glacé cherries, chopped**

method

1. Place butter and sugar in a bowl and beat until light and fluffy. Beat in egg, vanilla essence and milk and continue to beat until well combined.
2. Sift together flour and bicarbonate of soda and stir into butter mixture. Add hazelnuts, chocolate chips, coconut, sultanas and cherries and mix until well combined.
3. Drop tablespoons of mixture onto greased baking trays and bake at 180°C/350°F/ Gas 4 for 15 minutes or until golden. Remove to wire racks to cool completely.

. . . .
Makes 25

tip from the chef

Glacé fruits such as cherries or pineapple should be rinsed and dried before using in cookies to remove the sugary coating.
This helps to prevent the fruit from sinking to the bottom of the mixture.

original
choc chip cookies

■□□ | Cooking time: 15 minutes - Preparation time: 10 minutes

method

1. Place butter and sugar in a bowl and beat until light and fluffy. Beat in egg (a).
2. Add self-raising flour, plain flour, coconut, chocolate chips and hazelnuts to butter mixture and mix to combine (b).
3. Drop tablespoons of mixture onto greased baking trays (c) and bake at 180°C/350°F/Gas 4 for 12-15 minutes or until cookies are golden. Transfer to wire racks to cool.

Makes 35

ingredients

> 250 g/8 oz butter, softened
> 1 cup/170 g/5¹/2 oz brown sugar
> 1 egg
> 1¹/2 cups/185 g/6 oz self-raising flour
> ¹/2 cup/60 g/2 oz plain flour
> 45 g/1¹/2 oz desiccated coconut
> 220 g/7 oz chocolate chips
> 185 g/6 oz hazelnuts, toasted, roughly chopped

tip from the chef

Everyone's favorite biscuit, full of the flavor of coconut, toasted hazelnuts and a generous portion of chocolate chips!

a   b   c

malt
ball biscuits

■□□ I Cooking time: 15 minutes - Preparation time: 5 minutes

ingredients
> **90 g/3 oz butter, melted**
> **1/3 cup/60 g/2 oz brown sugar**
> **1/4 cup/90 g/3 oz honey**
> **1 teaspoon vanilla essence**
> **11/3 cups/170 g/51/2 oz flour, sifted**
> **100 g/31/2 oz chocolate covered malt balls, halved**

method
1. Place butter, sugar, honey, vanilla essence and flour in a bowl and mix to combine. Add malt balls and mix to combine.
2. Drop tablespoons of mixture onto lightly greased baking trays and bake at 180°C/350°F/Gas 4 for 15 minutes or until biscuits are golden. Stand on trays for 3 minutes before transferring to wire racks to cool completely.

....
Makes 25

tip from the chef
An obvious choice for a child's birthday party, these malty morsels will taste even better teamed with a malted milk shake.

jelly bean biscuits

■□□ | Cooking time: 15 minutes - Preparation time: 5 minutes

method

1. Place flour, sugar, vanilla essence, coconut and butter in a food processor and process until mixture resembles fine breadcrumbs. With machine running, slowly add milk and process to form a soft dough. Transfer to a bowl, stir jelly beans into mixture.

2. Drop tablespoons of mixture onto lightly greased baking trays and bake at 180°C/350°F/Gas 4 for 10-15 minutes or until biscuits are lightly browned. Stand on trays for 5 minutes before transferring to wire racks to cool.

Makes 30

ingredients

> 1¹/4 cups/155 g/5 oz self-raising flour, sifted
> ¹/3 cup/75 g/2¹/2 oz caster sugar
> 1 teaspoon vanilla essence
> 30 g/1 oz desiccated coconut
> 125 g/4 oz butter, chopped
> ¹/4 cup/60 ml/2 fl oz milk
> 185 g/6 oz small jelly beans

tip from the chef

Do not store different types of biscuits together as they will absorb flavor and moisture from each other.

candy
chocolate cookies

■□□ | Cooking time: 10 minutes - Preparation time: 10 minutes

method

1. Place butter, brown sugar, caster sugar and vanilla essence in a bowl and beat until light and fluffy. Gradually beat in egg.
2. Sift together flour, cocoa powder and bicarbonate of soda. Add flour mixture, candy-coated chocolates and almonds to butter mixture and mix well to combine. Cover with plastic food wrap and refrigerate for 30 minutes or until mixture is firm.
3. Drop tablespoons of mixture onto lightly greased baking trays and bake at 160°C/325°F/Gas 3 for 8-10 minutes or until cookies are firm. Stand on trays for 3 minutes before transferring to wire racks to cool.

Makes 30

ingredients

> 125 g/4 oz butter, softened
> 2/3 cup/100 g/3 1/2 oz brown sugar
> 1/2 cup/125 g/4 oz caster sugar
> 1 teaspoon vanilla essence
> 1 egg, lightly beaten
> 1 1/4 cups/155 g/5 oz flour
> 1/4 cup/30 g/1 oz cocoa powder
> 1 teaspoon bicarbonate of soda
> 125 g/4 oz candy-coated chocolates
> 75 g/2 1/2 oz chopped almonds

tip from the chef

Be sure to make biscuits a uniform size; not only will they look more attractive but they will also cook more evenly.

crazy cookies

■□□ I Cooking time: 15 minutes - Preparation time: 10 minutes

method

1. Place chocolate in a heatproof bowl set over a saucepan of simmering water and heat, stirring, until smooth. Remove bowl from pan and set aside to cool slightly.
2. Place butter and sugar in a bowl and beat until light and fluffy. Add flour and chocolate to butter mixture and mix well to combine.
3. Roll tablespoons of mixture into balls and place on lightly greased baking trays. Flatten slightly and press a chocolate or a caramel whirl into the center of each cookie. Bake at 180°C/350°F/Gas 4 for 12 minutes or until cookies are firm. Transfer to wire racks to cool.

ingredients

> 75 g/2¹/² oz milk chocolate
> 220 g/7 oz butter, softened
> 1 cup/220 g/7 oz caster sugar
> 1¹/² cups/185 g/6 oz self-raising flour
> 60 g/2 oz hundreds and thousands coated chocolates
> 60 g/2 oz caramel whirls

Makes 36

tip from the chef

A buttery shortbread biscuit base is the perfect foil for sweet confectionery decorations.

mocha
truffle cookies

■□□ | Cooking time: 15 minutes - Preparation time: 10 minutes

ingredients
> 125 g/4 oz butter, chopped
> 90 g/3 oz dark chocolate, broken into pieces
> 2 tablespoons instant coffee powder
> 2¹/2 cups/315 g/10 oz flour
> ¹/2 cup/45 g/1¹/2 oz cocoa powder
> 1 teaspoon baking powder
> 2 eggs, lightly beaten
> 1 cup/250 g/8 oz caster sugar
> 1 cup/170 g/5¹/2 oz brown sugar
> 2 teaspoons vanilla essence
> 125 g/4 oz pecans, chopped

method
1. Place butter, chocolate and coffee powder in a heatproof bowl set over a saucepan of simmering water and heat, stirring, until mixture is smooth. Remove bowl from pan and set aside to cool slightly.
2. Sift together flour, cocoa powder and baking powder into a bowl. Add eggs, caster sugar, brown sugar, vanilla essence and chocolate mixture and mix well to combine. Stir in pecans.
3. Drop tablespoons of mixture onto greased baking trays and bake at 180°C/350°F/ Gas 4 for 12 minutes or until puffed. Stand cookies on trays for 2 minutes before transferring to wire racks to cool.

....
Makes 40

tip from the chef
This is the biscuit version of the traditional rich truffle confection and tastes delicious as an after-dinner treat with coffee.

chocolate
pinwheels

■ ■ □ | Cooking time: 15 minutes - Preparation time: 15 minutes

method

1. Place butter, sugar (a) and vanilla essence in a bowl and beat until mixture is creamy. Add egg and beat until well combined.
2. Divide mixture into two equal portions. Sift 1 cup/125 g/4 oz flour into one portion and mix to combine. Sift together cocoa powder and remaining flour (b) and mix into other portion.
3. Roll out each portion between two sheets of greaseproof paper to form a 20 x 30 cm/ 8 x 12 in rectangle. Remove top sheet of paper from each and invert one onto the other. Roll up from longer edge (c) to form a long roll. Wrap in plastic food wrap and refrigerate for 1 hour.
4. Cut roll into 5 mm/1/4 in slices, place on greased baking trays and bake at 180°C/350°F/Gas 4 for 10-12 minutes or until lightly browned. Cool on wire racks.

....
Makes 30

ingredients

> **125 g/4 oz butter**
> **2/3 cup/140 g/41/2 oz caster sugar**
> **1 teaspoon vanilla essence**
> **1 egg**
> **13/4 cups/220 g/7 oz flour**
> **1/4 cup/30 g/1 oz cocoa powder**

tip from the chef

These are ideal last-minute biscuits, as the dough can be made in advance and kept in the refrigerator until needed.

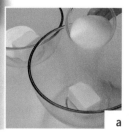

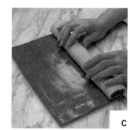

choc
layer biscuits

■ ■ □ | Cooking time: 15 minutes - Preparation time: 15 minutes

method

1. Place butter, brown sugar, caster sugar and vanilla essence in a bowl and beat until light and fluffy. Add egg and beat well. Sift together flour and baking powder. Add flour mixture to butter mixture and mix to make a soft dough.

2. Divide dough into two equal portions. Knead cocoa powder into one portion and malted milk powder into the other.

3. Roll out each portion of dough separately on nonstick baking paper to make a 20 x 30 cm/8 x 12 in rectangle. Place chocolate dough on top of malt dough and press together.

4. Cut in half lengthwise and place one layer of dough on top of the other. You should now have four layers of dough in alternating colors. Place layered dough on a tray, cover with plastic food wrap and chill for 1 hour.

5. Cut dough into 1 cm/^{1}/$_2$ in wide fingers and place on greased baking trays. Bake at 180°C/350°F/Gas 4 for 15 minutes or until biscuits are golden and crisp. Transfer to wire racks to cool.

ingredients

- > 250 g/8 oz butter
- > 1 cup/170 g/5^1/$_2$ oz brown sugar
- > ^{3}/$_4$ cup/185 g/6 oz caster sugar
- > 2 teaspoons vanilla essence
- > 1 egg
- > 2^3/$_4$ cups/350 g/11 oz flour
- > 1 teaspoon baking powder
- > ^{1}/$_2$ cup/45 g/1^1/$_2$ oz cocoa powder
- > ^{1}/$_2$ cup/45 g/1^1/$_2$ oz malted milk powder

....
Makes 40

tip from the chef

For a special occasion, dip the ends of cooled biscuits into melted white or dark chocolate and place on a wire rack until chocolate sets.

choc
almond biscotti

■□□ | Cooking time: 40 minutes - Preparation time: 15 minutes

ingredients

> **2 cups/250 g/8 oz flour**
> **³/4 cup/75 g/2¹/2 oz cocoa powder**
> **1 teaspoon bicarbonate of soda**
> **1 cup/250 g/8 oz sugar**
> **200 g/6¹/2 oz blanched almonds**
> **2 eggs**
> **1 egg yolk, lightly beaten, to brush**

method

1. Sift together flour, cocoa powder and bicarbonate of soda into a bowl. Make a well in the center of the flour mixture, add sugar, almonds and eggs (a) and mix well to form a soft dough.

2. Turn dough onto a lightly floured surface and knead until smooth. Divide dough into 4 equal portions. Roll out each portion of dough to make a strip that is 5 mm/¹/4 in thick and 4 cm/1¹/2 in wide (b).

3. Place strips on a baking tray lined with nonstick baking paper. Brush with egg yolk and bake at 180°C/350°F/Gas 4 for 30 minutes or until lightly browned. Cut strips into 1 cm/¹/2 in slices (c), return to baking tray and bake for 10 minutes longer or until dry.

tip from the chef

Biscuits may be partially dipped into melted chocolate for a two-toned effect. Before the chocolate sets completely, dip into toasted crushed almonds.

....
Makes 35

a

b

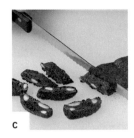
c

chocolate
macaroons

■ ☐ ☐ | Cooking time: 15 minutes - Preparation time: 10 minutes

method

1. Place egg whites in a bowl and beat until stiff peaks form. Gradually beat in sugar and continue beating until mixture is thick and glossy.

2. Fold cocoa powder and coconut into egg whites. Drop tablespoons of mixture onto greased baking trays and bake at 180°C/350°F/Gas 4 for 15 minutes or until macaroons are firm. Transfer to wire racks to cool.

ingredients

> **2 egg whites**
> **3/4 cup/170 g/51/2 oz caster sugar**
> **1/2 cup/45 g/11/2 oz cocoa powder, sifted**
> **11/2 cups/140 g/41/2 oz shredded coconut**

Makes 20

tip from the chef

Avoid baking these on a humid day as moisture will affect their texture.
Store macaroons in an airtight container in a cool, dry place.

christmas
tree cookies

■□□ | Cooking time: 12 minutes - Preparation time: 10 minutes

ingredients

> 185 g/6 oz butter, softened
> 1 cup/250 g/8 oz sugar
> 1 teaspoon vanilla essence
> 1 egg, lightly beaten
> 2¹/₂ cups/315 g/10 oz flour, sifted

method

1. Place butter, sugar and vanilla essence in a bowl and beat until light and fluffy. Gradually beat in egg.
2. Add flour to egg mixture and mix until just combined. Knead dough into a ball, wrap in plastic food wrap and refrigerate for 45 minutes or until firm.
3. Roll dough out on a lightly floured surface until 3 mm/¹/₈ in thick. Using a Christmas tree cutter, cut out cookies and place on lightly greased baking trays. Bake at 180°C/350°F/Gas 4 for 10-12 minutes or until pale golden. Transfer to wire racks to cool completely. Decorate cookies with icing and sweets if desired.

....
Makes 30

tip from the chef
If you find the dough sticky or difficult to handle, chill it a little longer or roll it between sheets of nonstick baking paper. Don't add extra flour to the working surface as this will spoil the texture of the biscuits.

christmas
stocking biscuits

■□□ | Cooking time: 10 minutes - Preparation time: 10 minutes

method

1. Place butter, icing sugar, egg, plain flour and self-raising flour in a food processor and process until a soft dough forms. Knead dough briefly, wrap in plastic food wrap and chill for 30 minutes.

2. Roll out dough on nonstick baking paper to 5 mm/1/4 in thick. Using a template of a Christmas stocking or a Christmas stocking cookie cutter, cut stocking shapes and place on a greased baking tray. Bake at 180°C/350°F/Gas 4 for 10 minutes or until biscuits are golden. Transfer to a wire rack to cool.

3. Dip tops of stockings in dark chocolate to make a 1 cm/1/2 in border. Allow to set.

4. Dip biscuits into milk chocolate half way up dark chocolate. Allow to set.

ingredients

- > 125 g/4 oz butter
- > 3/4 cup/125 g/4 oz icing sugar
- > 1 egg
- > 1 1/4 cups/155 g/5 oz plain flour
- > 1 1/4 cups/155 g/5 oz self-raising flour
- > 90 g/3 oz dark chocolate, melted
- > 60 g/2 oz milk chocolate, melted

....
Makes 24

tip from the chef

Use any leftover melted chocolate to pipe designs onto the stockings, if desired.

christmas
butter cookies

■□□ I Cooking time: 12 minutes - Preparation time: 10 minutes

ingredients
> 375 g/12 oz flour
> 2 teaspoons baking
  powder
> pinch salt
> 250 g/8 oz butter,
  cut into pieces
> 2 eggs
> 220 g/7 oz caster sugar
> 1¹/2 teaspoons vanilla
  essence
> 1 teaspoon finely grated
  lemon rind
> 1 egg white, lightly
  beaten, to brush
> plain or colored sugar
  to decorate
> assorted cookie
  decorations

method
1. Sift together flour, baking powder and salt. Rub in butter with fingertips until mixture resembles breadcrumbs. Make a well in center of mixture.
2. Beat together eggs, sugar, vanilla essence and lemon rind, add to flour mixture and mix to make a soft dough. Knead lightly on a floured surface and cut into 4 pieces. Wrap each in plastic food wrap and chill for 3 hours.
3. Preheat oven to 180°C/350°F/Gas 4. Roll out one piece of dough at a time to 5mm/¹/4 in thick and cut into desired shapes. Brush shapes with egg white. Decorate cookies as desired.
4. Arrange cookies on lightly greased and floured baking trays and bake for 10-12 minutes or until cookies are firm and edges are golden. Cool on wire racks.

....
Makes 48

tip from the chef
Use the picture as a guide and decorate cookies as desired before baking. Or bake plain biscuits and decorate with icing after cooling.

zimtsterne

■□□ | Cooking time: 10 minutes - Preparation time: 10 minutes

method

1. Preheat oven to 180°C/350°F/Gas 4.
   Stir together icing sugar, almonds, caster sugar, lemon juice and egg whites to the consistency of short pastry.
2. Place dough between sheets of plastic food wrap and roll out to 5 mm/1/4 in thick.
   Cut out shapes using a star-shaped cutter and place on paper-lined baking sheets.
3. Bake for 10 minutes or until golden. Cool on wire racks.

ingredients

> **200 g/6 1/2 oz icing sugar, sifted**
> **200 g/6 1/2 oz ground almonds**
> **60g/2 oz caster sugar**
> **squeeze lemon juice**
> **2 egg whites**

....
Makes 50-60

tip from the chef

These famous Swiss cookies also result delicious if the almonds are replaced by hazelnuts, or a mix of both of them is used.

cheese daisies

■□□ | Cooking time: 15 minutes - Preparation time: 15 minutes

method

1. Beat cheese and butter until creamy. Sift together flour, paprika, salt and black pepper and stir into creamed mixture with sesame seeds. Wrap dough in plastic food wrap or foil and chill slightly.
2. Preheat oven to 180°C/350°F/Gas 4. Press dough through a biscuit press fitted with a flower nozzle onto ungreased baking trays. Roll little balls of dough in poppy seeds and push into centers of flowers. Bake for 12-15 minutes or until golden. Cool completely.

....
Makes 30

ingredients

> **125 g/4 oz mature Cheddar cheese, finely grated**
> **185 g/6 oz butter, softened**
> **185 g/6 oz flour**
> **1 teaspoon paprika**
> **1 teaspoon salt**
> **1/4 teaspoon freshly ground black pepper**
> **2 tablespoons toasted sesame seeds**
> **poppy seeds**

tip from the chef

Keep a batch of unbaked dough in the freezer and shape and bake when needed.

cheese-pecan
crisps

■□□ | Cooking time: 15 minutes - Preparation time: 10 minutes

ingredients

> 1/2 cup plain flour
> 1/2 cup self-raising flour
> pinch of salt
> generous pinch of ground chilies
> 60 g/2 oz butter
> 1 1/2 cups finely grated tasty cheese
> 1/2 cup finely chopped pecans
> 2 tablespoons beer or water

method

1. Sift flours, salt and ground chilies into a bowl. Rub in butter with fingertips until mixture resembles breadcrumbs. Stir in cheese and pecans (a). Add beer or water and mix into a dough. Chill for 30 minutes.

2. Roll dough out thinly on a lightly floured surface. Cut into small rounds (b). Arrange on lightly greased baking trays and bake at 180°C/350°F/Gas 4 until crisp, about 15 minutes. Cool on a wire rack.

Serves 6-8

tip from the chef

For the crisps not to be extremely hot, use seedless ground chilies.

sesame
pepper crackers

■□□ I Cooking time: 10 minutes - Preparation time: 15 minutes

method

1. Place rice flour or plain flour, sesame seeds, sage and peppercorns in a bowl and mix to combine.
2. Combine mascarpone and Cheddar cheese. Add cheese mixture to dry ingredients (a) and mix to form a soft dough.
3. Turn dough onto a lightly floured surface, knead briefly and roll into a sausage shape. Wrap in plastic food wrap (b) and refrigerate for 40 minutes or until firm.
4. Cut into 1 cm/¹/₂ in thick slices (c), place on lightly greased baking trays and brush with egg. Bake at 190°C/375°F/Gas 5 for 10 minutes or until biscuits are golden and crisp. Transfer to wire racks to cool.

Makes 30

ingredients

> 1 cup/185 g/6 oz rice flour or 1 cup/125 g/ 4 oz plain flour, sifted
> 2 tablespoons sesame seeds, toasted
> 1 tablespoon chopped fresh sage or 1 teaspoon dried sage
> 2 teaspoons pink peppercorns, crushed
> 125 g/4 oz mascarpone
> 60 g/2 oz mature Cheddar cheese, grated
> 1 egg, lightly beaten

tip from the chef

Unsalted and buttery, with a fat content of 90 per cent, mascarpone is made from cream. If it is unavailable, mix one part thick sour cream with three parts lightly whipped double cream, or beat 250 g/8 oz ricotta cheese with 250 ml/ 8 fl oz single cream until smooth and thick.

a

b

c

index

Introduction 3

Basics
Basic Biscuit Recipe 8
Cinnamon Crisps 6
Coffee Kisses 10
Night Sky Cookies 14
Thumb Print Cookies 12

Energizing
Carob Hazelnut Macaroons 20
Golden Oat Biscuits 18
Montecarlo Biscuits 22
Wholemeal Carob Chip Cookies 16

Choc Chips
Chocky Road Biscuits 24
Giant Choc Chip Cookies 26
Original Choc Chip Cookies 30
Rich Choc Chip Cookies 28

With Candies
Candy Chocolate Cookies 36
Crazy Cookies 38
Jelly Bean Biscuits 34
Malt Ball Biscuits 32

Chocolatey
Choc Almond Biscotti 46
Choc Layer Biscuits 44
Chocolate Macaroons 48
Chocolate Pinwheels 42
Mocha Truffle Cookies 40

Festive
Christmas Butter Cookies 54
Christmas Stocking Biscuits 52
Christmas Tree Cookies 50
Zimtsterne 56

Savory
Cheese Daisies 58
Cheese-pecan Crisps 60
Sesame Pepper Crackers 62